Heaven's Drumhead

Poems from a Blessed Drummer

Heaven's Drumhead

HERB McCLEES

Poems from a Blessed Drummer

FallingGecko
PUBLISHING

P.O. Box 896, Kirkland, WA
98083-0896, U.S.A.

Heaven's Drumhead

Poems from a Blessed Drummer

Herb McClees

1st Edition
Copyright © 2014 by Herb McClees

ACKNOWLEDGMENTS
Some of the poems first appeared in the chapbook: *The Catch* (2008), FallingGecko Press, Kirkland, Washington. The poems: *Beauty's Work, The Scarf, Scenes in the Park, Debutante Ball;* and *Shopping Cart Cowboy* were first published in the anthology: *Poetic Reflections At The Creekside (2013)*, Clark Crouch, Editor, Creekside Poetry Publications, Woodinville, Washington.

Cover art, by Joan Tarbell Plato was inspired by the poem "Eagle Pass". Author photo is from Todd Boyle's video of the Duwamish Tribe's 2013 First Nations event.

Information and Permissions from:
FallingGecko Publishing
P.O. Box 896, Kirkland, WA 98083-0896
www.FallingGecko.com

ISBN-13: 978-1500553654
ISBN-10: 1500553654

Printed in U.S.A.

For Arvelle

TABLE OF CONTENTS

I. HEART - *the drum of life*

II. COMMUNITY – *dancing to drums*

III. ART - *a drum circle*

IV. BEING - *distant drums*

V. SPIRIT - *a blessed drummer*

I. HEART

the drum of life

Hoof Beats

In my dream, I was on a plateau
Overlooking a somber plain;
Towards a dawn that was slow to come;
And in the distance, lightning played.

Far off, heading my way,
Was a lone rider;
Riding hard across the limbo land
From Forever to Now.

How brave! How vulnerable!
He could be struck by the first bolt
Hurled by the impending storm;
Yet, he rides on.

As he drew nearer, I could see the rider
    more plainly, his face shadowed
    and mysterious;
And I could hear the tha-rump, tha-rump
Of his pony's hooves…

Then the nurse came in
To check my wife and the fetal monitor.

(Could she hear my heart,
Beating wildly, as we waited?)

children's laughter
from the rooftop —
crows and gulls

Scenes in the Park

A man sprinting,
Towards children leaping,
   in bronze;
Followed by a little girl,
   who toddles off —
To a bed of flowers.

***

Sitting on a bench,
A little boy to his dad:
   "A great way to watch football!"
His reply: "No, it's baseball."

***

At the beach waiting:
Three little girls in swim suits,
While a man inflates a small boat,
   on his knees.

Mr. Happy

There is a family made of bronze
At the neighborhood mall:
A woman and two small children,
Set on the edge of the fountain pool;
In the plaza next to the cinema.

She sits with her back to the water,
Her daughter, legs akimbo next to her;
They are watching her son,
Standing on the edge,
His arm, extended toward the
    dancing water;
His face, shining in exuberance.

Then, a real family meets the one
    in bronze:
The boy (tee shirt saying "Mr. Happy"),
Jumps up on the edge of the pool
And strikes the pose of his twin;
His father (tee shirt proclaiming
    "Mr. Cool"),
Without slowing, says "Come along."

Singing Girl

A beautiful singing girl,
Dressed in red
With blonde, bobbing curls;
Crosses the lid-hot street.

The song lives through her:

In her lithe step, the rhythm;
Her arms' swing, the melody;
And in her petticoat's flair,
    the cymbals' brush.

At her feet, dust swirls in cloudlets;
As a crumpled playbill tumbles by,
    which pauses every now and then...
As if smelling rain, far off,
    in the freshening breeze —
And then bounces on,
    hopping a dry gutter.

Debutante Ball

A rambunctious cotillion
   of dubious belles,
Rung too soon or too late,
Encircles and dissipates
   in colorful clutter and flimsy pretense.

After the debutants' presentation,
Stirring music (and a drink or two)
Effects a magical transformation
From gala ball to naval review.

The dancing throng becomes
   an ensign fleet
Maneuvering before an admiral's flotilla
   anchored in the bay!

Each maiden ship is under the
   gallánt command of a junior officer,
Who must tack his new vessel,
   hands on,
And issue crisp orders,
   (not always obeyed, and sometimes
   unheard)
Over the martial music of the escadrille
Playing for a crenellated line.

In the spectator fleet, retired captains
   and wives,
Hold their spy glasses high;
And study their bonny ship's quick turns,
Braced with a tonic of pride and anxiety.

Some ships' courses are sailed with grace,
While others are cut perilously close,
Requiring a hard turn to port,
Or suffering a bump amidships
    (or worse, torn rigging or sails)!

As the spectacle ends, the vessels
    are returned by lieutenants
    eager for a new command;
Save for one buccaneer heart,
    who heads out to sea
Sailing his first prize
    and captured crew!

Devastation

There is something to tell,
Something inside
Which bites and gnaws,
Grappling rib cage walls;
Sleeping fitfully.

There can be no peace,
While it tears at my bones,
Till flesh turns clay;
And clay dust.

Then write:
Here lies One Victim
    of nuclear Holocaust,
Soul seared by spirit-star heat,
Killing all living ideas
    and builded memories;
Leveling towers raised
    to hope and life,
And extinguishing the very sun
    and sky;
Leaving no one to savor the blue
Warmed by the sun's fire.

The Fairy Queen

In sunshine and firelight,
In harvest and healing,
In passion and heartache;
The Queen's radiance shines.

She surges nature's verdant tide,
And the colt's prancing gait;
And warms the healing waters
Drawn from secret springs.

***

She lives in singing dancers
Circling her roaring bonfire,
And dies with the setting sun
Streaming across quiet lakes.

Upon her fairy smile
Lovers leap, hand in hand,
Fiery heights, unscathed;
To find their own hearts, ablaze.

***

At last, her fire to ashes falls
With coals glowing as distant stars.
Her open heart to the immured calls
As birdsong heard through prison bars.

Silent man, stricken with remembered pain,
'Tis by the Fairy Queen's death that love
    trumps grief,
Then meet her gaze!, her awestruck
    champion,
And leap the sunset glow;
    and your queen — reclaim!

The Lady Grey

Let me go, let me be!
Let me sail the wide, wide sea:
With its wild waves slippin' any hold.
Let me go, let me be!
Let me sail the wide, wide sea:
For its warm embrace, however cold.

2
And I prayed it to be!
As I sailed the wide, wide sea:
For a ship, swift and yare, races won.
Then, I prayed it to be!
As I sailed the wide, wide sea;
And my soul, with the sea…
    danced as one!
(Chorus)

3
Through the glass, I did see,
While I sailed the wide, wide sea:
In the spring, Her bright flag
    on the heights.
Through the glass, I did see,
While I sailed the wide, wide sea:
In the fall, bonfires on starry nights.
(Chorus)

4

'Tis by grace, I am free!
Long, I've roamed the wide, wide sea:
On the Lady Grey, I wait the tide.
'Tis by grace, I am free!
Long, I've roamed the wide, wide sea;

And yet — the green hills call:
   "Home, abide!" *(repeat line)*

(Chorus)

Yare: Nimble, lively, maneuverable. Glass: Spyglass.
Lyrics for song composed by author.

Horace

A candle's flame dies to be reborn,
Its light, a karmic dance.

I lost my stepfather years ago,
A gentle man and poet.
I was there when he died;
But, did I really know him?

What if we could meet again,
Breaking the rule of time,
Flying kites as boys and striving as men;
Would we ever true friendship find?

To know this man who has gone before
I turned to family and friends
Who recalled his open spirit,
Which in sharing, never ends.

Bereft, I searched my memory
And walked her echoing halls
For a sight of him, or a voice…
   "Not in here" was all.

***

Outside those walls, I sadly roamed
In twilight gardens, beyond time,
Till I found a motley throng;
And in their midst, a fire sublime.

"I am lost!" I cried.

"Welcome friend!" a tall man shouted,
    opening the crowd.
Before him stood a brazier
Holding an opalescent fire
Fed by vestal tenders and
    my mother, now young!

"For Horace" she sighed.

After a silence, an ancient,
    stirring the coals, inquires:
"And friend, what bring you?"

"Myself", I replied.

"And have you brought *all* of yourself?"

His words hung in the somber air —

"As far as I know", I answered weakly.

"Bring your 'all' and you can join us,
For what you seek is in your life,
    "lived out";
And adding, as he resumed his task,
    "and yours has some ways to run."

***

And so, I bade Horace's devotees
    farewell;
For "finding him" in this life
    or in the next was not the question;
More the reverse: "allowing Horace
    to find me".

In the perpetual twilight,
A weariness descends — and sleep;
Then honorable surrender
To an old soul homing within.

I awoke from my pilgrim quest,
With a cutting from an old tree:
My stepfather's life, still growing,
    informing my art and my love;
And the will to "live out" my life
    in all its "ways to run";

And so live on, and so live on.

sunny garden...
under her straw hat
twilight and dancing stars

Kingdom of Words

At dawn, I explore you
With the back of my hand,
Hoping to reclaim by gentle caress,
Territory already lost
In our kingdom of words.

***

Already, they desert us;
Words and messengers, yours and mine;
Save our old servant, Touch,
With your message: "I am thine."

***

Upon news of the enemy's advance,
Faithful Touch brings a living prayer
And hope for communion
   when all words fail.

***

The enemy will not parley,
Our kingdom may be lost.
But, if we must surrender… know this:
While they can hold us
      Incommunicado,
We are already free!
Holding each other,
      Totally.

Arvelle's Story, a Dance Narrative

Once upon a time,
There was a little girl in the country
Who loved watching birds
Soaring high in the sky,
And imagined herself flying —
    on eagle's wings.

The vibrant colors of
Daisies, tulips, roses
Put sparks in her feet
    that carried her skipping
    and bobbing around her garden
Like the finches she had raised.

She dreamed of dancing
In shows and ballet
With her name in lights —

    [on point]

However, her undisciplined body
    cried "No!"

    [stumbling]

But, her stubborn spirit cried "Yes!"
And she took up tap instead,

Which brought her
    to dance for our Lord —
The Lord of all dances.

One of her celebrated dances
   was for little children
Who put stars in her eyes,
   and hope in her heart,
Whom she loved as her own.

For them, she collected teddy bears,
Which she cleaned and blessed
That a fireman or policeman could give one
   to a child in crisis.

New dances followed;
But, over time began to slow
With each passing day.
Her words became fewer...

Even so, she made cards
With pictures she took
Of neighborhood flowers
Speaking for her... folding them ...

After many folds...

After many folds... many folds... folds
   many... fold... after many folds

[Pause for stillness and silence]

[Slowly begin to dance, gradually grow bigger]

[Stand in center with scarf out and say:]

   after many folds
   origami bird
   offered to the wind...

[Run with scarf as if on eagle's wings, big smile and exit]

Note: Narrative developed in collaboration with Kristin Kissell to accompany her dance performance at memorial service for Arvelle McClees (1946-2010) at St. John's Episcopal Church Kirkland, WA on March 26, 2011.

Passion Light

Years ago, I walked down an ancient hall,
With a candle for a light;
My hand guarding a fragile flame,
That flickering, drew me to its glow.

I saw a fairy dancing on a shining lake,
Dressed in blue with bright yellow hair;
In leaps and fancy steps,
    she spun a dervish tale,
Before a foot lighted shore, unaware
Of her audience touched by
    her passion light.

My charmed hand still feels that dance,
In sinews warmed to the bone;
My hearth, though, is now home to snow;
And a chill wind makes its moan.

I must go down that hall again;
But with my own inner light
One that flows from hand to heart,
And that in my own dance shines
Till I see the kindled glow
In another's glistening eyes,
And joining hearts, we watch the snow.

Applause

The lines we spoke
In our traveling play
Were not our own.
Our glistening bodies spoke for us,
Without touching,
Joined under the tropical sun.

For weeks we toured,
Town to town, mostly waiting:
Hot days and humid nights,
Without rain,
Performing under slow-turning fans.

Reviews were, at best, mixed;
And so, after a steamy performance
We bid adieu, hand in hand,
To an empty house,
And the applause of rain
On a metal roof.

The Scarf

She visits him once a year in the fall
When the raking is nearly done,
To catch-up and pass the time.

Far off, in the chilly dawn,
Birds trill as she speaks;
Standing or kneeling (there is no bench);
She brings news of the family, the kids;
    and her garden;

Pausing from time to time,
    (clipping here and there);
She finds more to say,
In response, perhaps,
    to a quiet question or a memory's tug.

As the sun clears the distant trees,
She lays her own work aside,
    a scarf of remembrance:
Made from the threads of their lives;
Knit with words remembered and said
    from dawn visits over the years,

A warming scarf against
    the coming winter;
And now, having mended its snags
    and pulls... she can wait and dream.

Before long, catching the morning light,
A bright red and orange maple leaf,
Cartwheels into view to rest
Near a small flag which
    unfurls and furls;

And then, she feels her hair
    being gently stroked;
As their days, months, and years,
    together and apart,
Rank on rank, pass in review,
In honor of Life's veterans.

II. COMMUNITY

dancing to drums

Ancient Clock

In my dream, I was a bird
    in a flock,
Suspended between earth and sky;
With strong wings beating in synchrony;
And compass: migration's pull.

We were the living works of an ancient clock:
Its pendulum, our spring-fall swings,
Its chime…
    a far-off thunderclap!
        echoing, echoing…

My flock! —

And falling,
    falling…
        in tighter circles;

Powerless to call back
The gunshot from the hunter's blind.

Inspired by slam challenge words:
"dream", "echo" and "blind".

quiet restaurant—
the waitress remembers
our favorites

Shopping Cart Cowboy

1

We round up carts and head 'em out,
   on endless asphalt plains;
And drive 'em to market,
   in a clatter of wobbly wheels.

Chorus
I'm a shopping cart cowboy
   on another roundup drive;
We herd 'em to the feed lots,
   where they're stuffed to bust their sides.

Yippy yi yea, yippy yi yo;
Punchin' steel to stay alive!

2

Though feed lot rustlers nab 'em,
   we bring every dogie home;
And most times, steel ribs showing,
   I must trail 'em back, alone.
(Chorus)

3

After bedding down my herd,
   I sing lonesome to the stars
When dogs howl or sirens wail,
   I double with my guitar.
(Chorus)

A shopping cart cowboy!

Tune: "Ghost Riders in the Sky"

Foolscap

Surprised wisdom
Crumpled in a banana-gold crème
Without a scorched leaf
Blown from a blasted tree.

Sing in sepulcher tones of enchantment,
Clear and gold blent
In a symphonic statement
Void of sentiment.

Plush times these:
Fused in welded swatches
Pasted together from donuts and coffee;
And super-sports GTO's and Wildcats.

Bring silence, timeless silence
From the fomenters of youth,
Chasing a ragged corpse
Down echoing streets
Into suburbs of middle age.

A shout, terrific vocal-magic
Rips to pieces the velvet shroud
Prepared for thy head.

But, what is this, this statement
Leaded in red
On yellow foolscap?
Mere words to stuff into the wind ripped
Cracks of an old building,
Whirling in darkness.

property listings—
behind the broker's window
a trapped moth

Crystal City

"Location, location, location!" cried the ads,
  "Sky on all sides!"

Crystal City's story begins at Hub Park,
Where the city's broad avenues radiate,
  like spokes on a wheel;
And where ground was broken
  for the "City in the Sky".

The ceremony was held at the monument
  at the center of the park;
There, the bands played and stirring speeches made
Before a stone sculpture, broody and dark.

Few liked the unsigned work's rough, imperfect shape;
And the rest, not surprised to learn that the sculpture
  was a gift;
But, all were puzzled by its title: "Founding Stone."

One pastor at the groundbreaking,
In his prayer-speech, compared the stone to the one
Rejected by the builders of the temple,
  that later became the cornerstone;
At this point, some in the crowd,
  (mostly developers and investors), fidgeted;
But the tension was relieved by a child's stage whisper:
"What's the big deal? It's just a broken rock."

After the ceremony, construction began
Starting with the alabaster avenues;
With their chalk-white, crenellated walls;
And for the skyscraping towers, foundations laid.

All that can be said about the fabrication method used
    is that it is both elegant and fast;
Capable of building structures of fractal beauty,
    from damp, freezing air; virtually, "overnight".

Then, one afternoon, the "City in the Sky"
    was complete:
Unique and splendid, as it slowly revolved
    in the winter light;
With its straight-edged towers
And open sky bridges, high overhead.

Sunlight refracted through its crystal spires
Played multiple rainbows on the icy walls
Lining its bone-white avenues,
    now tinged with gold.

But, sadly, the next morning,
The "City in the Sky" sailed into balmy air;
And its bridges, streets and commons
    began to sag, then melt into ponds;
And its proud towers collapse into icy lakes,
Before its first citizens could take possession.

Crystal City's founding stone?
But a grain of common dust;
That in freezing weather,
Seeds a crystal of ice;
And with other crystals, joined
    in intricate repetition;
Founded an enchanted world, hidden—
    in a flake of snow.

At the Dance

Saturday night swing dancing
    at the "Third Place Commons";
As I arrive, a handicap mini-bus pulls up,
    blocking the crosswalk.
I walk around it...

Tonight, a polka band,
    the "Smilin' Scandinavians";
The place is already jumping.
The "usual suspects" are here,
Including the man who leads bands
    from the dance floor
With scissor-like arm movements.

In the roped-off area, children dancing:
    solo, in pairs, and trios,
Or encircled by parent's arms;
And babies, too, gently rocked
    to the beat.

Behind them, a skinny girl (7 or 8),
    and future ballet star,
In pink jeans and a pink jersey top
Practices her jetés accompanied
    by the "Pennsylvania Polka".

A smiling lady in her eighties,
    stands and watches;
Her frail beauty hinting nobility.

The band leader introduces the band,

He plays accordion and sings —

My father had an accordion,
when I was small...

And is backed by a banjo, drums;
    and a tuba's reliable oom-pah.
Rounding out the band, a clarinet,
    played with a klezmer touch.

On the sidelines, a young, Chinese couple
Is intently learning the polka,
    one step at a time.

A women rolls her wheel chair over to me,
In her face, I could see the signs;
I ask her name: "Sharon"
    and tell her mine;
But, soon a trim, female aide retrieves her.
Later, I spot them on the dance floor.
Sharon's arms are raised and swaying,
    as she claps to the beat.

Next on Sharon's dance card,
A black-haired man,
Who guides her chair in figure eights
    to the "Blue Skirt" waltz.
He has the following dance, too.

After that, a broad shouldered,
    hunchbacked woman cuts in.
She rolls Sharon's chair
    back and forth,
Both are beaming;
Sharon's in heaven, clapping her hands.
Though she may not be
    "all there",

She is certainly
  "all here".

Now, the Frail Beauty and
  her slim, white-haired partner,
Join the swaying throng,
They dance to "cut a rug".
His quick grace and precision
  recalling Astaire's.

  I see my father's hands
  on the keys and buttons ...

Is Life's secret before us
  in this Brueghel village tableaux?
Ignore for the moment,
  the decrepitude of some dancers
Or the diminished minds of others;
Instead, feel their movement,
See their faces, their eyes; and
Imagine how they must feel as the elixir
  of dance and community
Works its magic.

My father had an accordion,
I see his hands on the keys and buttons;
But he never played it,
When I was small.

The Third Place Commons: community-focused mall
in Lake Forest Park, WA

Friends of the Library

Cars inch along,
Outpaced by pedestrians;
City blood flowing
Through village veins.

At the hub, the library,
With people in radial flow:
Teens with skateboards, boomers
    with laptops
And mothers with children in tow.

On its terrace
A new statue stands:
An old man transfixed,
Listening.

At his feet are bricks,
Memorials set in stone,
And around him voices
From Friends of the Library.

Soldiers

Patriots
Recruited,
One by one.

Soldiers
Marching
To the drum.

In foreign lands,
Falling,
One by one.

Across America
Bells rung,
One by one.

We answer ours
For our soldier son.

Fallen.

Fallen.

Fallen.

a man with two lattes
walks with his friend,
swinging on crutches

Leaf Blower

I awoke to birdsong
A blessed sound
And decided to take an early walk
    in the slanted light
To drink in the dewy peace.

But tranquility was broken
By the ripping snarl
Of a leaf blower,
Riding the back
Of a "lawn care specialist."

Back and forth he swept —
Without apparent effect
For the debris was soon reclaimed
    by the wind
For another day.

Could this sound be demonic,
Extolling in its stumbling gait
    futility;
And suppressing thought?

But when I drew close
He throttled it back,
    to a chuckle;
And the smiling specialist
Waited for me to pass.

This humble man, too,
    had been swept away,
Across the border,
By winds of economic change.

Now, I know what this sound means,
A phrase from long ago,
It is the "sound of freedom"
And he heard it in Mexico!

Note: "Sound of Freedom" – U.S.A.F. term for jet fighter's roar.

Borders

We are a frame shop.
We protect your picture
And guide the viewer's eye
Whether a family portrait
Or priceless work of art.

This couple's van Gogh,
A too familiar print,
How can it be framed
So their friends will see it
For the first time?

Border it with a textured matte
And place in a gilded frame,
All, to guide the eye
From our clamoring world
To a wheat field in Arles,
Not so long ago.

Now, an art collector and physician
Brings a photograph to frame
Taken in Africa.
Another, too familiar, scene:
Malnourished children
With big smiles,
Waiting at a clinic.

How can it be framed?
How can we guide the eye
To this scene of pain and joy?
No frame will do!

A dry mount should suffice
To, as printers say, "Let it bleed."
Then entitle it: "Sans Frontières",
"Without Borders."

E Pluribus

Stone by stone
Brick by brick,
A strange city
Comes to town.

Face by face
Child by child,
A new crowd
Shops the mall.

Word by word
Voice by voice,
Distant lands
Shape our tongue,

In which we sing America,
And our plea to Thee:
We are many, make us one!

Note: "E pluribus unum" – from many, one.

The Silent Ones

To land in our cacophonous world,
The visitors required silence,
    about five minutes of silence,
So our leaders told us to hush and be still.

I remember hearing the cat purr
    on the other side of the room
And the faucet drip in the kitchen.
For a time there was silence, all around.

Silence wrapped the reception center
And the mute parade of leaders
    and celebrities
Waiting for our first guests.

But to the visitors, there was still noise,
Not from the air conditioning
    which had been shut off,
Or the stray bird's chirp in the rafters;
But from the hosts: a droning buzz
    of clamoring thought –
The five "W's" and an "H" et cetera;

And so, the visitors returned to their craft.

*Rudyard Kipling's "Six Honest Serving Men", from his years as a
journalist: "Who", "What", "Where", "When", "Why" and "How".*

III. ART

a drum circle

The Catch

The fisher poet spins his soul
Into a gossamer line;
And then with costly bait
Casts into a misty sea.

On shore, he waits
        to feel a tug;
And, fearing break,
        plays his line,
Dancing with the unknown,
        to safely net
His most precious catch:
        two hearts:
The reader's
        and his own.

Pan

How shrill his music
Like shattered glass
Scattered on an airy main!

Pan plays on,
His golden curls
Dancing wildly;

Now, lifting his pipes
To the blazing sky;
And then,
With a laugh,
Playing softly
To the black earth.

Robin's Song

Our songs have been sung.
We listen and wait
At the bottom of the year.

Brave robin,
Harbinger of spring,
Sing for us a new song,

One shaped by ancient dawns,
And composed this starry night
For spring's first morn.

after many folds
origami bird
offered to the wind

from the tree

a black handkerchief falls—

crow magic

maple leaf print
    yellow and brown on stone
artist's proof

Her Portrait

Just go and see her portrait set

On earth, where form and life are met,

And praised as touching heaven's joys;

Now time's slow work with lead alloys;

Not touched, the title on the frame,

Etched in gold, her eternal name.

An acrostic, for St. Valentine's Day.

"Beauty for Ashes"

In the fall
Beauty passes
and
remains.

Inspired by Katherine Todd's painting,
"Beauty for Ashes", acrylic & copper on canvas.

Beauty's Work

Beauty glimpsed in fabric, drape and form;
In cutting, stitching, sewing expressed;
For a moment, can be touched,
    when worn,
In the admiration of her dress.

Some would hold Beauty cheap
    and sell her dear
As the latest fashion, haute couture, for a diva
    (to Beauty a stranger, though near) —
A prop for her drama, a lure.

But for many, Beauty is sweated
    in fittings and alterations,
Is present in a sewing machine's ticking
    while children, nearby play;
Is felt in a mother's devotion
    and a daughter's adoration;
And lived in her labor, oblivious
    to the tick-tock of fashionista stilettos.

*In Laura King's art sewing machine stitches are used
to outline fashion design sketches.*

Desert Workshop

I have the strangest workshop
To fashion my latest poem.
It is far out in the desert
And I must find it every time!

There, I work with broken tools
Using scraps found in the bin;
Yet, I have more than I need
And the silence I require.

Where is this workshop, you may ask?
Now, my tale gets even stranger.
My workshop is within,
Not marked on any map!

When I am empty of words,
And have faced my desolation,
I can enter my soul's desert;
And, freely, become lost.

In time, my workshop finds me!
And I craft another poem,
Unexpected, yet longed for;
Written in the nick of time!

Sea Message

Our ship sails, bearing our lives
   to the four winds;
Its wake, quickening the sea's foamy skin.

O crescent-seared sea,
   flaked with the sun's scattered embers;
Quench not the failing light!

I was a camera awash in beauty,
   suspended between sea and sky;
And powerless to act.

Then came the shutter press,
   a sea hawk's stoop, down scarlet canyons…
Towards the metaled waves.

At the graceful dawn,
My pen took flight…
Across the glistening page,
Damp with the wind-borne message
   of the sea.

cold moon climbs misty mountain
first sleet on dry leaves...
whispers and brush strokes

A Pen's Dream

My pen dreams ... and traces
    reveries in uncertain memory,
And spears flotsam thoughts
    tossing on mythic seas,
    freed from retail packaging.

But to be real, to remain,
The pen must dream on the page
    while being lightly held;
 And thought unwound
    from its silken cocoon
Without breaking its gossamer strand.

This precious strand is spun
    into lines of inky words,
And wondrous fabric made;
Only then, by sewing and cutting
Can we fashion and bring to life
    the stuff of dreams.

Absent the spinner's gentle hand
Or a tailor's steady grip,
An eager pen held carelessly
Can become a rapier;
And by thrusting this way and that,
Rend the liminal matrix that separates
Writer from whirling darkness.

As for me, I prefer writing shorter verse:
Less chance for my wounded pen
To bleed its words or worse, pierce the page;
And open windows that cannot easily close.

unfurnished dream house
buyer to write description:
many windows, many doors

The Old One

Under a chilling moon,
A stormy, patchwork sky
Pivots upon an ancient tree.

Rooted in heaven, the Old One chants,
In silhouette and runic branch,
His ringed heart's saga:
Recalling flashing storms,
The music of birds and Spring's deep pull.

The Enchantress Moon, not of this earth,
Casts a baleful eye; and jealous,
Halts time with her Mesmer gaze.

She blazes, setting limbs with silver fire;
And with Boreas, makes
      a frozen fountain raise;
While within his crystal prison,
The Old One sings on.

The Moon, now a dragon's eye,
Shapes the gnarled tree
Into an awful fretwork
Burning into the sky.

The moment warms …

That-Which-Is, comes with a crash –
      primeval,
Cracking the marble sky
      into fragments!
And the Old One sings on!

Lakeside Reflection

Dawn

Two suns: one above, one below;
The lower one, unquenched in still water.

The double light blinds,
My wide brim hat can't ward
  the second sun's rays;
And yet, I am transfixed
  by the otherworldly sight
As if, I had seen two suns before.

Perhaps, a stranger's beauty-gasp
  pins me thus in reverie;
From another time, another place —
  maybe even, another life.

Now, *that* would be "tele*vision*"
  worthy of the name;
And inspiration, too, for poetry…
  without words.

***

A wizarding breeze furrows the lake;
And with airy passes, spells the second sun
Into a dazzling school of golden fish
  flecked with green;
Which in leaping play and
  with freshening wind,
Dissolves into swarms of burning bees,
  then diamonds.

Noon

His conjuring complete,
The wizard presents to the ascendant sun
    a living work:
For his fabulous dining board,
A cerulean blue and silver brocade.

Evening

A coppery sky cools
    over the royal blue table;
The rich brocade swept away,
Replaced by the sheerest of veils
To which jewels are fixed
    as stars appear.

***

A spangled veil is spread upon the lake,
And a gracious breeze adds a smoothing shake
While evening guests settle on tented shores;
And table set for souls and stars to partake.

Night

The velvet darkness embraces
    departing guests,
Stilled by the splendor of the Milky Way;
And holds them, while they behold
    the starry treasure,
Spilled across heavens above
    and below.

IV. BEING

distant drums

The Skater

He skates on the surface of things,
Smooth words on ice;
His tongue,
A flashing blade,

Carving graceful arcs,
With remarks
Pitched, just so,
To bite and hold,
Yet glide,
Over what swims below;

Always on point,
Holding,
Yet letting go.

Flying

To fly without a destination
Without a flight plan
Is irresponsible,
And can only be explained
As the act of someone
Who loves flying
More than
Landing.

Growth

The
more
I grow
The less
I know,
For in the end
I become the world entire;
And cannot see that I am held
In the hands
of
Love.

shattered beer bottle —
paper label
holds it together

Lies

Enigmatic correspondence...
With an answer in plain sight.
Is this the answer or a sacrificial lie
To put off, mislead, and hide;
And if the truth is here,
Is it hidden steganographically;
Must the messenger's head be shaved?

Guard!

Steganography: the art of hiding a message inside another message.

another year
weathered fence
the nails' rust streaks

Time

The ticking of a clock
Encompasses a *world*
    of duration and intensity.

Each tick... a hammer's knock;
    precise,
        formed in time

With a depth of sound
    trailing...
        endlessly...
          away.

TICK.

Behold, a single Moment
    in the desert of Time,
Whose metallic spire
    catches the noon blaze
In glinting fire.

Far away,
    on the world's edge...
Is another Moment such as this!

TOCK.

Between these adamantine towers
Stretches leveling sand,
Baked by a never-setting sun.

Storm Bird

Dark skies pierced
By ragged white swords.

Flashing in and out
Of existence,
Against the sky,

An albatross,
White as snow.

With each stroke,
He reappears,
Higher and higher.

waiting for the doctor's knock —
the fan's hum
my shallow breathing

A Gentleman at the Door

"There's a gentleman at the door, Sir."

"Who is he?"

"Death, Sir."

"Did you tell him that I am not at home?"

"I did, Sir; and he agreed, that is why
he is waiting."

In Hands

In hands, cupped hands;
In darkness, radiant darkness;
In indwelling warmth, a mother's breath;
In the slightest breeze, a feather's
    tipping stroke;

In tears, an ocean's wave's break;
And in the salt air from far off,
    the fragrance of green.

Vermont Solitude

I

"Goodbye. Good luck," I say
As their car backs and turns
And is swallowed by a dark bend in the road.

The moon reappears
Having sailed, somehow, into
     a cloud-locked bay;
But the night is cold,
She won't prolong her stay.

"Yes, I know *you* are here too."
The wind rubs its back against the trees
     stretching perhaps,
Then pads across the lawn
     into the woods and is gone.

Still, I am not alone.
My friend remains, despite the cold,
Relishing one might say
The night's blues and grays.
Touched now and then by silver.

He doesn't talk much
Even for a New Englander.
Instead, looks off towards the woods;
And beyond them, to a rock littered pasture
     in Vermont
Tilting steeply behind a farmhouse.

Smoke rising from a chimney
   for some, signals friendship.
He would dissent and watching the thin column
   wind upwards
Evaporating before reaching the level
   of the circling hills
Read the word spelled in the smoke's ascent
   as "loneliness."

II

Once, I walked among those hills,
And wanted to climb one of them,
   claimed by a farmer's hand.
There was a house, weathered gray;
   and near it, a car;
And from a chimney, smoke curled.

I knocked on the door...
Surprised no one had seen me come.
For not many do come, at least on foot;
But drive by
   in summer, to shop for antiques in the towns;
   in winter, to ski in the mountains.

I knocked again... no one at home.
They must have another car, or truck, perhaps;
And being Saturday, the family has gone
   to the village to market and gossip,
   leaving dinner to simmer on the stove;
But in the country, an unattended fire
Can grow to consume an entire house
   before help arrives.

I waited awhile for their return,
Watching two spotted kittens playing
    in the yard;
Then walked up their hill, anyway,
Looking over my shoulder from time to time.

The sun slipped behind a ridge
Before I had gone more than halfway;
    and I walked down
Stopping by again to see
If they had come back from town.

They hadn't.
Though now I could see a light was on.
Was there a light before?
Maybe they had never gone;
But silent behind the door
Waited for my steps to fade,
Not hankering for company.

Earth Song

Open my eyes, my heart
To yours, Earth;
That my life may sway
To your song.

Sometimes, you sing very slowly
Or your voice breaks...
Sometimes your words
Run together,
Or the music won't come.
Yet, even then, I must know
Your heart's song.

(Could your feelings
Be a mother's
Who watches her children go,
Or a lover's
When the embrace must end?)

If there can be no words,
Then let me feel your tears
In the warm summer rains.

Let hear your sigh
In the restless wind;
And see your caress
In the swaying tree,
Or in the broad acres' grassy waves.

But, most of all, Earth
Let me hear your lover's call.

over sunny lake
two birds circle and dive…
bright dapples remain

keyboarders pause
in the library —
the rain squall's soft roar

Sound of Silence

That awesome sound of silence
Rushing, hushing,
overflowing,
Streaming over thoughts;
Into mind,
Mindless of itself.

Epitaph

Where the heart no longer beats
Time cannot flow.
Where a man no longer breathes
The wind cannot blow.

A soul is laid in stillness
Among dark leaves,
And winter's chillness
Is all that breathes.

V. SPIRIT

a blessed drummer

At the World's Edge

At the world's edge
One man climbs.

His comrades await,

    Weather bound.

Hounded by the wind
Incessant and icy,
He is bone cold and weary.

    Each step wounds.

But, in the inchoate chorus,
A Voice...
Welcomed within.

    Then the world drops away...

The summit is won.
Unblinking stars shine
In the inky blue.

    His wounded heart sings.

park drinking fountain
overflowing...
two workers, kneeling

Living Water

Refrain
I love your Living Water
Washing down from skies above.
Pour it over my thirsty spirit
Fill me with your Living Love.

When lost though not forsaken,
A prisoner of my fear;
May my thirst be for Living Water
Even though my end be near.

(Refrain)

I place my heart before You,
Lift it up to skies above.
Fill it with your eternal Spirit,
Never quench my burning love.

(Refrain)

Lyrics of hymn composed by author.

O, Holy Spirit

O, Holy Spirit, transform us in Christ;

To accept His love, and love one another;

Grant us strength and grace, for our walk in His light;

Alive in His Word, a light for our brother.

Descending Dove

"This is my Son, whom I love;
with Him I am well pleased."

1

The blessing of his father's love
Fell on Jesus at the river;
Holy Spirit as gentle dove,
Our Messiah to deliver.

(Refrain)
The lesson of the descending dove
Is to do the Lord's bidding,
Outstretching wings, upheld by love;
In the Spirit flying.

2

In love, baptized, we can not fail,
Living for our Savior's purpose;
Though storms may blow, we surely sail,
When the Lord is our true compass.

3

Born to fly, we must fall to know,
God's abiding love, upholding;
Our leaps in faith, help
        strong wings grow
For young spirits, still unfolding.

Scripture: MT:3:16, MK 1:9.
Lyrics of hymn composed by author.

St. John's Angels

Stand up, standup for Jesus;
Our angels sing his song;
Without bright swords or armor
They stand with his most strong;
The voices pure of children,
Lift high, hope's dancing flame,
That lights the way before us;
So we may live his name.

Stand up, standup for Jesus;
And hear his healing words,
That mend the broken hearted,
Sung sweeter than the birds;
From lips of St John's children,
Our future robed in blue;
A glimpse of heaven's treasure,
For you and you and you.

Dedicated to the children's choir of St John's Episcopal Church of Kirkland, WA, "The Blue Angels".

Inspired by "Standup, Standup for Jesus" by George Duffield Jr (1818-1888).
Tune: "Morning Light" by George James Webb (1803-1887).

Little Ones

Chorus:
Long ago, I heard Him call:
"Come to me, come to me";
From the crowd, we heard His voice:
"Come to me, my children".

1
"We can't see you! We're too small!"
To find the One who calls.
"Do not hinder them!" He said;
But, lead them here instead.

2
Blessing us like family,
He held us in his arms.
Why does Jesus care for me,
And love us "little ones?"

3
Then, He told the crowd about
God's Kingdom, with a smile;
It belongs to each of us,
Who's "like a little child."

(Chorus)

Scripture: MK 10:13-16
Lyrics of hymn composed by author.

Judgment

By and by I will be called
To judgment before His throne;
My soul in balance weighed
By the King I've barely known.

And I am guilty before the law
For the case is open and shut!

Would that He, His only Son
My shepherd advocate be
And whose name my lips confess;
But, does He know me?

And I am guilty before the law
For the case is open and shut!

If there can be no pardon,
Then, O King, parole me to your Son,
To be a black sheep in His flock,
Touching hearts more tender than my own.

The Raised, the Praised

The raised, the praised, the newly dead
Asleep, and yet must walk
In ragged files down mossy aisles
In somber procession.

Silently, from all time
The sleeping dead are drawn
Through velvet glens and grassy fields
To a sparkling sea of light.

Set in a shadowed valley
    shaped like cupped hands,
The great candlelit assembly
Embraces the pilgrim dead;
Celebrants in dancing waves
Bearing them to its heart.

With alleluias pouring down
    again and again;
The sleepers are baptized anew,
Until the raised, the praised,
Quickened, can answer the multitude's chorus:
    "For all the saints";
And then, swooning in wonderment,
The pilgrims, responding:
    "For all the saints ... alleluia!"

As dawn breaks, the last trump!
Sounded from without,
Resounding from within!
Arise, fainting hearts,
For the King of Kings is here,
Arise!

Shepherd Lord

1

Shepherd Lord, Emmanuel;
Now, I travel life's hard road;
Nourished by your Gospel Word,
Strengthened so, to bear my load.

Refrain

Jesus, Lord, you died for us;
   Love is why, love is why;
Guide us on our journey home;
   By our side, by our side.

2

Help me hear a stranger's tale,
   or invite new company;
Pilgrims all, we're heaven bound,
Home, where we are family.

3

Fearless Guide, and loving Lord,
When the path is steep and slow,
Let me climb where you have trod;
Save me from the rocks below.

4

On my right, my holy Guide;
On my left, a grieving friend;
On both sides, my Lord's with me;
Now, and at my journey's end.

Coda

Our Shepherd calls! Thy kingdom come!
Alleluia, alleluia;

[Refrain]

Alleluia, alleluia, alleluia!

Lyrics of hymn composed by author.

Harvard Yard street sign:

Divinity Avenue:
Private Way

Before the Word

God's Holiest Name can't be spoken,
Being formed of the Silence,
    before Creation,
Before, even, time itself;

Silence with a brooding
    Immanence —
Living Silence from before
    the Beginning,
Before any   thing;

Preceding the Singularity
    and the First Light;
With its Almighty Sound
    (the "Big Bang").

Could this "ur-silence" be the matrix
On which the Word was spelled,
Hurling the fabric of heaven
    into space and time;

Which, settling over billions of years,
    Is bestrewn with stars;
And near one of which, at least,
    the question raised?

A revisioning and expansion of the first part of
p181 "The Church of His Holiest Name".

Biblical references: JN 1:1; 1 KG: 19:12; and RV 8:1

The Jug

Morning

Another drinking party last night,
   (Thought the jug;)
While my rich master kept me filled
All the travelers sought my company.

At the oasis I was passed around
    mouth to mouth.
My wine loosened their tongues
And the men boasted and sang.

I awoke, empty and cracked,
Discarded by my master.
Unable to hold wine, new or old,
My serving days are over!

Noon

Though I ache with new cracks,
Am I not the same jug praised
For its intricate design
(and my master's fabled grape)?

But, who am I,
Now empty and cracked?
Philosophy replies:
   "The essence of a jug: its 'jugness'
     is its ability to contain."

Well, I am empty
And I can still contain;
But not all things,
Not with my cracks.

So I'm a jug that can't hold drink;
But can hold sand?
His scholar's words have not
Helped me at all!

Here I am, cast away,
To be filled with sand!
Already it drifts around me
As it falls down the dune.

Night

A faint humming sound:
Like a flute or a chorus; but from where?
Surely, I am alone in the desert
The caravan has moved on.

Still the sound grows louder
It comes from within:
Music made by a cool wind
Blowing across my mouth!

Now Wisdom whispers:
    "Your emptiness is key"
And from within, the Master speaks:
    "Your worn, imperfect shape is your
        voice.
My Messenger breathes your words!"

Flag Dancer

For the boy a broom handle
Was enough to spin the world,
With nimble fingers —
A game of momentum and gravity,
    letting go and catching,
Falling around a center, scribed in air.

"Why not add colored flags?" I ask.
            "I would like that" he said.
"Why?"
            "Because of the sound."

A huge flamingo flock wheels in flight
    Over Lake Victoria;
And long ago, a buoy bell ding-dongs,
As I bring my dinghy about, her sail luffing.

"I would like that. "

Blue
When I next saw him, he had added a scarf,
    pale blue silk, lent by his mom,
And was intently twirling his broomstick flag.
Blue for the sky, for space, for other worlds
For the caveman's bone toss in "2001"
For freedom.

White
On another day he was spinning his pole
Outfitted with a snow-white flag,

Air caressed the flag, and drew it out,
And furrowed its silk with a thousand fingers.
With each orbit, he grew more to feel
Her resistance and acceptance
In an ethereal embrace.

White for the wind that waves all flags
In war and peace and in Olympic games,
Flags, ringing their halyards at the UN Plaza,
     nearly two hundred,
And flying prayers in Tibet, a million.

Red
His skill improved with each passing day,
Now, he could twirl his broomstick baton
     over his head;
And even toss and catch it.
Today, he wields a red flag in a corrida display
That could arouse Pamplona's proudest bull.
     Olé!

Scarlet for the robes of the bishop
Who slapped me at confirmation,
According to tradition,
When I was the boy's age;
Not hard, but deliberately,
A "buffeting" for mindfulness
Or "to drive out the devil" some would say.

"This is His blood shed for you,"

Yet, His church burns with Pentecostal flames
And is not consumed.
     Hallelujah!

Green

This time his baton had a green silk scarf
The color of Indonesian waters years ago
When my Dutch ship en route to Singapore
Waited in Belawan's roads for a launch
    to transfer refugees:
Two families climbed lowered stairs
    (the children had sun-blond hair!)

And far out in the Malacca Strait,
Passing whales sang familial
    and individual songs
Heard by kin many miles away
    in their global migration.

Yellow

Today, I saw his recital performance
The flag dancer's baton had a
    bright yellow square
Conjuring school buses and caution lights;
Do I stop or do I go?
And wheat fields, ripe pears and the
    lure of gold –

Whose heaviness weighs me down
Pulls me, sinking, falling, down
    "Ashes to ashes dust to dust"
Falling forward to rebirth
As the prayer wheel turns –
    "To turn, turn will be our delight."

Now, the valley bells' tinkling clangor
    and the winds buffeting,
And the myriad prayer flags:
Blue, white, red, green and yellow;

Together, transforms an old spirit
   on his road to Everest.

I am now a boy.

Eagle Pass

O surrounding, countless chorus,
We are joined in celebration;
Fellow creatures of the Spirit,
All naked under heaven.

The cicadas' voice, thin and dry,
Fills the air of our sacred ground;
On a bluff, exposed and high;
A place for our drums' healing sound.

In the west, I can see,
By the Buck Moon's light,
Twin Mesas' silhouette;
    and – the Pass.

But, as I watch, they fade to scrim;
Diversions for my brooding thoughts
    on the study: "Incidence
    of Alcoholism in
    Single Parent Tribal Households,"
Presented today in Council.

But, the drum circle works its magic;
And thoughts fade into musings,
And soon, I am surfing drumbeat waves
With turtle shell rattles' insistent frisks,
    the spray.

Around me: dozing elders,
Mothers singing softly, to little ones,
    snug in their arms;
And, ah yes! quiet children,
Teenagers hushed in dreamy silence.

The drum rhythm begins to change,
     assuming a "lame-horse" gait,
A spell-caster: hypnotic and sky reaching;
Even the stars begin to sway,
     then to dance in waves,
Rippling heaven's drumhead!

Now, slow drumming begins,
Beaten from the heart,
          (hard won!)
Folded with the Spirit,
          (bless the drummers!)
The drumming morphs into a lullaby,
          (forgotten, yet familiar);
Which the women, begin to sing;
          (some, chant into the darkness);

And joining them,
          (do you hear?)
Crossing-River, my mother!

The Milky Way's ghostly band
Sweeps down beyond the mesas,
Over the road through Eagle Pass
For an old spirit's journey,

Someday soon, someday soon.

My Ashes

To Barbara S. who shared her wish.

I want my ashes scattered
   on Mount Rainier;
I want them carried to the top
   and— cast to the winds;
So their almighty broom
   will sweep them into the clouds;
And Boreas can mill them
   into dust.

Then, I want each grain of dust,
   irregular and dark,
To be redeemed by the dew,
   attracted to its rough shape;
And through a freezing art,
Make the broken grain the heart
   of a fragile snow flake:

    Unique and white,
      slowly
     spinning,
    as   it
       sidles
   down
      ward,

Spelling in its geometry,
   an unheard crystal harmony;
Or, in warm air, that a grain of dust
Seed a water droplet, for a "bit of cloud."

***

I would like to float with these cloudy bits,
   too small to fall,
In a wisp of the mountain's sentinel cloud;
Suspended, between earth and sky;

And be there when the cloud
   is blown east by a Pacific front;
And ride with them on its airy river
   in drifting reverie
Over jack pine covered foothills;
And then the sere grasses of the prairie —

And where, when it meets a cold front
   from Canada;
I am shaken awake by their turbulent congress
   in time to witness the birth of a
      great storm:
     reaching
     into the
     stratosphere;
Patrolled by flashing lights
   and rolling thunder!

At the heart of the storm: droplets dancing,
Caught in a vertical game
   of pitch and toss;
And growing heavier with each rise and fall,
'Til at last, with countless more,
   too big to float, they begin to fall
     to earth;
Or, in a downdraft, be driven from heaven;
Here, in a cloudburst with battering hail;
Or there, in an April shower, as small rain.

Rain to soak the parched fields
   of the Palouse;
And, to pelt the back of another boy,
   emerging from a pool,
With such vigor, that he, too,
Will look up and behold
   The thunder cloud,
      dark and churning
         with a greenish hue;
And chilled in its downdraft,
Remember the smell of lightning
    and the sting of hard rain.

***

And with that rain,
   I too,   would fall,
Lost in my liquid guise;
To roll down slopes in gravity's thrall;
And grow by tributary absorption,
Into a trickle, then a rivulet,
   before cascading into a creek;
And joined by various waters;
   swell the onward flow:

One stream might have the turquoise tint
   of rock flour from a far off glacier;
Or, a drainage ditch might bear algae blooms
   of spectral green,
Fed by runoff from industrial farms.

***

Months later, water bearing specks,
   of my finest dust, will arrive
      at the mouth of the Columbia;

And passing through the great river's
   proud, rolling wave;
Will catch the western sun in its breaking curl –

Before falling into the Pacific;
To be gathered up and held
   by the immense ocean, the mother of life;
For a millennium or two —
   before again,
     being let go.

And, if that's not to be,

Then, I would settle for Paradise!

Boreas –   *In Greek mythology, god of the north wind.(bow RAY us)*

Sentinel Cloud – Reference to the flattened cloud associated with high
                 mountain peaks.
Congress –   *Sexual relations.*

Palouse –   *Eastern prairie region of Washington State.(pah-LOOZ)*

INDEX OF FIRST LINES

A Word about the Author

Herb McClees, a Northwest poet, came to Seattle, from Texas, via Singapore and Boston. He appears at local "open mics" and is a member of PoetsWest, Redmond Association for the Spokenword, and Haiku Northwest. His poetry performance has been selected for broadcast on KSER-FM.

Mr. McClees' first published work was his 2008 chapbook: *The Catch*, FallingGecko Press. More recently, several of his poems were included in *Poetic Reflections at the Creekside* (2013), an anthology of Northwest "open mic" poets.

A poet of the community, Mr. McClees was invited to read at the Duwamish Tribe's 2013 Columbus Day First Nations Celebration; and on another occasion to celebrate the return of weekly live-music swing dancing at a local mall.

Herb McClees began writing poetry at fourteen; but life in Dallas in the fifties didn't suit him. All changed when his mother married an expat manager in the oil industry, for his next posting was Singapore! Herb was enthralled by its multi-racial, polyglot atmosphere, trading port bustle; and the gung-ho party life of the small American community.

After graduating from the Singapore American School, Herb McClees returned to the U.S. to earn an engineering degree from M.I.T., taking electives in philosophy and humanities to balance his major's heavy math and physics requirements; and furthering his love of language and the imagination. There, he was particularly influenced by Dr. Huston Smith (*Religions of Man*), who taught Eastern religion.

In poetry, Poe, Whitman, Sandberg, and Eliot were early influencers, and later, Chinese poetry, Frost, Yeats, Thomas, Millay, Wallace Stevens and Baudelaire.

16018867R10081

Made in the USA
San Bernardino, CA
15 October 2014